Don't miss these other record-breaking books!

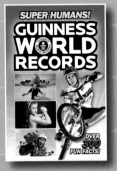

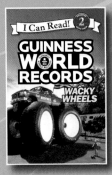

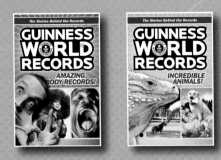

GUINNESS WORLD RECORDS

AWESOME ENTERTAINERS!

by CHRISTA ROBERTS

HARPER
An Imprint of HarperCollinsPublishers

Guinness World Records: Awesome Entertainers!
© 2016 Guinness World Records Limited
The words GUINNESS WORLD RECORDS and related logos
are trademarks of Guinness World Records Limited.
All records and information accurate as of December 1, 2015.

ISBN 978-0-06-234169-3

Design by Victor Joseph Ochoa
Layout by Kimberly Shake
16 17 18 19 20   PC/RRDC   10 9 8 7 6 5 4 3 2 1
❖
First Edition

Guinness World Records holders are truly amazing, but all attempts
to set or break records are performed under controlled conditions
and at the participant's own risk. Please seek out the appropriate
guidance before you attempt any record-breaking activities.

TABLE OF CONTENTS

INTRODUCTION

Anyone, anywhere, has the potential to be a record-breaker! For over 60 years, Guinness World Records (GWR) has timed, weighed, measured, verified, and documented thousands of the world's record-breakers in every category that you can imagine. There are over 40,000 current records!

Record-breaking is free to do. If the GWR adjudicators (the official judges who confirm records) approve your idea for a new record—or if you can prove you've bettered an existing title—you're on your way to becoming Officially Amazing!

Awesome Entertainers! features act after act of amazing artists who have earned a Guinness World Records title— over 100 of them. Swallowing swords, singing upside down, cheerleading, and more—these entertainers strut their stuff right into the record books!

Just think, maybe you—or someone you know—will be motivated to step into the spotlight to go after a record of your own after reading about these real-life record-breakers!

> Remember, many of these record-breakers are trained performers with years of experience—always check with an expert before attempting any dangerous records.

No clowning around, the performers you'll meet in these pages are some of the most impressive on the planet. Whether it's a spectacular act that's part of a circus show—or one that deserves to be—these world record holders have officially entered the entertainment big top!

LADIES AND GENTLEMEN, BOYS AND GIRLS . . .

At age 12, **Norman Barrett** from the UK joined the circus . . . and never left! This ringmaster for Zippos Circus holds the record for the **longest career as a ringmaster**, marking 57 years of entertaining the crowds in 2014. You could say the circus runs in his blood, as his father owned the circus!

HE'LL BEND OVER BACKWARD!

Talk about flexible! Australian **James Loughron**, aka Aerial Manx, traveled in a backbend position over 65 feet in 7.81 seconds at the Venetian VIP Show on January 10, 2015, achieving the **fastest human backbend walk**.

A human backbend consists of only the participant's hands and feet touching the floor, with the arms extended above the shoulders and head, and the back completely arched.

That's not James's only talent either: he also holds the one-minute record for (gulp) the **most backflips while sword-swallowing**: 20!

TWISTS AND TURNS!

Leilani Franco, a contortionist based in the UK, holds the record for the **fastest time to travel in a contortion roll**—covering 65 feet in 17.47 seconds. She started with her feet on the ground before arching her back and rolling forward on her chest. She also holds the record for the **most full body revolutions maintained in a chest stand position in one minute**—29! In a chest stand, a person rests their body facedown on the floor, bending their legs over the head so that the feet rest on the floor in front of the face. In order to count as a full revolution, both legs must complete a 360-degree revolution before returning to the original starting position. It's no wonder that one of Leilani's nicknames is Bendy Girl!

AN APPLE A DAY . . .

Sliced apples are a great snack—but you might be surprised at how **Johnny Strange** slices them. The UK entertainer holds the record for the **most apples held in one's own mouth and cut by a chain saw**. His chain saw buzzed through eight apples in one minute and never once missed the target on October 12, 2013, at the Doncaster Racecourse in South Yorkshire, UK. Now that's what you call a close shave!

DON'T MOVE!

Fellow UK daredevil **Daniella D'Ville**—aka Danielle Martin—put her trust in **Johnny Strange** on October 12, 2013. That was the day that the two set the record for the **most apples held in the mouth and cut by a chain saw**, cutting through 12 apples. This "slice of history" also took place at the Doncaster Racecourse.

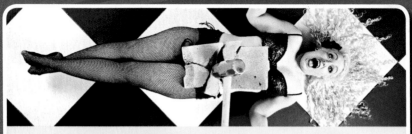

SMASH TIME

Can you imagine lying on a bed of nails with a concrete block placed on your torso? Not the most comfortable position—but that's how **Daniella D'Ville** achieved yet another world record—this time with the **Great Gordo Gamsby** of Australia. Gordo hit the block on Daniella's chest with a sledgehammer to break it into pieces. In fact, he broke 16 blocks, the **most concrete blocks broken on a bed of nails in one minute**, on the set of the TV series *Lo Show dei Record* in Milan, Italy, on June 26, 2014.

NO STRANGER TO DANGER

Johnny Strange didn't waste any time at the Doncaster Tattoo Jam in South Yorkshire, UK, on October 12, 2013. He achieved the **fastest time to break 16 concrete blocks on the body of a female**, doing it in 30.40 seconds with his willing partner, **Daniella D'Ville**, who had the blocks smashed on her. The extreme entertainer likes to push boundaries, saying, "I love being able to show people something they've never seen before."

HOT SPIN

Also performing at Wonderground in London, UK, on September 14, 2012, **Pippa "The Ripper" Coram** of Australia spun three burning Hula-Hoops simultaneously while performing the splits. The artist kept the hot hoops spinning around her arms and neck for more than 10 seconds, and earned the world record for **most fire hoops spun while in splits position**.

ULTIMATE FACT:
Not only does Pippa twirl Hula-Hoops—she makes the hoops herself! The hoops have wicks around the perimeter and are soaked with gasoline to light them.

DEFYING DEATH

The **Great Gordo Gamsby** holds the record for the **most fire clubs juggled while sword-swallowing**. Gordo managed to juggle three blazing fire clubs for the required minimum of 10 seconds while swallowing a sword at the Wonderground circus show in London, UK, on September 14, 2012.

ONE WHEEL, TEN CHAIN SAWS

Riding a unicycle is a special skill. But riding one while juggling 10 chain saws? That was amazing enough to earn **Chayne Hultgren** of Australia a record for **most chain-saw-juggling catches on a unicycle**. Also known as the Space Cowboy, Chayne performed this terrifying feat on the set of *Officially Amazing* in Sheffield, UK, on July 20, 2015.

HEAD GAMES

Don't invite **Burnaby Q. Orbax** and **Sweet Pepper Klopek** over the next time you're baking cookies. . . . The Canadian siblings—a duo known as the Monsters of Schlock—hold the record for the **most baking trays buckled over the head in one minute**. In all, they totaled 55 trays in Niagara Falls, Ontario, Canada, on August 31, 2012.

HOLD YOUR TONGUE!

No cat-and-mouse game here: **Casey Severn** achieved the **most mousetraps released on the tongue in one minute**. In the set time, a staggering 53 traps were snapped on his tongue at the Maryland Renaissance Festival held in Crownsville, Maryland, on October 12, 2014. This beat the previous record by six traps!

SNAP TO IT

Australia's **Zoe L'Amore** (aka Zoe Ellis) is the female record holder for the **most mousetraps on the tongue**. She "licked" the competition by releasing 24 traps in a minute!

"SWORD" THROATS

Natasha Veruschka of the USA holds the female record for the **most swords swallowed simultaneously**. She swallowed 13 swords on September 3, 2004, at the 3rd Annual Sideshow Gathering and Sword Swallowers Convention in Wilkes-Barre, Pennsylvania.

Following in Natasha's footsteps, the **Space Cowboy**, aka Chayne Hultgren of Australia, claimed the record for the **most swords swallowed simultaneously by a male**. He swallowed 24 blades on September 12, 2012, at the Guoman Hotel in London, UK.

OPEN WIDE

On Sword Swallowers Awareness Day
(February 28, 2009), New York City
resident **Natasha Veruschka** did
something no one else has done:
gulped down a 22.83-inch
blade, the **longest
sword swallowed**.
Now that's hard
to swallow!

CRACK THAT WHIP

On April 11, 2009, on the set of *Lo Show dei Record*, in Italy, **Adam Winrich** of the USA used a bullwhip to achieve the **most drink cans whipped in three minutes** by taking out 23 cans. For this record, a bull or stock whip can be used. The cans were replaced on a specially designed pedestal by two assistants every time they were broken. Adam is no one-trick pony when it comes to whipping up Guinness World Records titles. He also holds the records for **most candles extinguished by a whip in one minute**—102—and **cracking the longest whip** (216 feet)!

HONEY, I HAVE AN IDEA . . .

Patrick Brumbach's wife certainly trusts her husband. . . . She was willing to let him throw knives around her in order to achieve their record—and it paid off. The **most knives thrown backward around a human target in one minute** is 63, achieved by the German couple in Schloß Holte-Stukenbrock, Germany, on August 17, 2011. Patrick actually threw 71 knives, but eight were discounted.

GULP

The blade known as the **Sword of Swords** has been gulped down by 40 of the world's best-known sword-swallowers, making it the **most-swallowed sword**. It was made by British stunt performer Thomas Blackthorne in 1994 as a symbolic icon to link an otherwise solitary and disparate community. The Sword of Swords has been swallowed by several record holders, including the **most tattooed man**, Lucky Diamond Rich of Australia, and Natasha Veruschka, who you've already met (pages 17 and 18).

STAND TALL, WALK FAST

Ashrita Furman of the USA knows his way around a pair of stilts. In fact, he completed the **fastest mile on stilts** in 12 minutes, 23 seconds at the Queens College running track in Flushing, New York, on August 29, 2008. But that wasn't his first experience with greatness. On December 17, 2004, Ashrita covered 4.97 miles on stilts on the Huan Dao Road, Xiamen, China, in 39 minutes, 56 seconds, making him the **fastest stilt walker over 8 kilometers** (5 miles). This beat the previous record—unchanged for *112 years*—by 2 minutes, 4 seconds, traveling at an average speed of 7.53 miles per hour.

THESE STILTS ARE MADE FOR WALKING

Once **Saimaiti Yiming** of China started off on his stilts, he kept them on for 24 hours and completed a distance of 49.4 miles, walking around Shanshan County, Xinjiang, China, from September 30 to October 1, 2003: the **farthest distance on stilts in a day**. How high was he? Well, his stilts measured 28.7 inches from the ground to his ankle. And they weighed 22 pounds!

BACK IT UP

The **fastest tightrope backward walk over 100 meters** (328 feet) is 1 minute, 4.57 seconds, and was achieved by Italian circus acrobat **Maurizio Zavatta** (pictured) on the co-filming set of *CCTV—Guinness World Records Special* and *Lo Show dei Record* in Kaifeng, Henan, China, on May 20, 2014. For this outdoor attempt, Maurizio went head to head with tightrope performer **Aisikaier Wubulikasimu**, from Xinjiang Province in China, whose best result was 1 minute, 6.06 seconds.

However, Aisikaier can still lay claim to the **fastest 100-meter** (328-foot) **tightrope walk** while facing forward, with a time of 38.86 seconds achieved on June 6, 2013, in Wenzhou City, Zhejiang Province, China.

FIRED UP

Professional fire-eater and circus sideshow entertainer **Carisa Hendrix** of Canada can claim the **longest duration fire torch teething**, lasting 2 minutes, 1.51 seconds on the set of *Lo Show dei Record* on April 12, 2012. In fire torch teething, the artist must use their teeth to grip a flaming torch and hold it upright without using the hands.

FLAME FILLERS

The **largest human image of a torch** consisted of 3,032 participants and was achieved by the **National Integrated Forum of Artists and Activists** in Karnal, India, under the coordination of its chairman, Pritpal Singh Pannu, on March 23, 2014. With this record, the youth organization wanted to highlight the evils of corruption.

FLIPPED OUT

Italian **Michael Martini** is the **youngest person to achieve a quadruple somersault**, at the age of 13 years, 196 days. He performed the head-over-heels feat during rehearsals at Circo Orfei, in Massafra, Italy, on June 1, 2013.

Michael is trained by René Rodogell, a member of the Flying Rodogells, a well-known Mexican family of acrobats. Michael's sister Angela performed her first triple somersault at age 13. Michael and Angela are part of the flying trapeze troupe the Flying Martini, and their parents are also both circus artists. A real family act!

PLAYING WITH FIRE

The **most fire torches lit and extinguished in one minute** is 83, achieved by **Preacher Muad'dib** (pictured) of Ireland in Potters Fields, London, UK, on Guinness World Records Day, November 18, 2010. Making this record especially tricky is that only two torches can be used during the attempt—these must be put out and lit again during the event.

Preacher also formerly held the title for **most fire torches lit and extinguished in 30 seconds** but this was claimed by **Heidi Bradshaw** from the UK on July 4, 2014. Better known by her stage name Snake Fervor, Heidi ignited and put out fire torches 59 times, beating Preacher's total by six.

If a fire breaks out when **Hubertus Wawra** of Germany is around, don't be surprised if he steps in to help. That's because he can claim the **most torches extinguished in 30 seconds with the mouth**: 39. He achieved this feat on the set of *Guinness World Records—Ab India Todega* in Mumbai, India, on February 21, 2011.

RIDING TALL

Edgard Zapashny, **Aleksandra Blinova**, and **Kristina Gritsaenko** of Russia formed the **tallest human pillar on moving horseback** on June 17, 2011, in the arena of the Sochi State Circus in Krasnodar, Russia. All members of the Zapashny Brothers Circus, they stood on each other's shoulders and let go of each other's legs while the horses trotted around the arena. The trio used safety harnesses but no form of support.

DRILL DOWN

The **longest metal coil passed through the nose and out of the mouth** measured 11 feet, 10.91 inches and was achieved by Las Vegas sideshow performer **Andrew Stanton** on the set of *Lo Show dei Record* on March 31, 2012. Andrew, who performs as Mr. Screwface, chose to pass the greased metal coil through his nose and out of his mouth using a power drill. Getting a filling at the dentist suddenly doesn't seem so bad!

HOOKED ON RECORDS

Burnaby Q. Orbax of Canadian stunt act the Monsters of Schlock achieved yet another record to make you squirm, at the Essex Fun Fest in Ontario, Canada, on July 11, 2015, by lifting 80 pounds. Doesn't sound too heavy? Well, this was the **heaviest weight lifted using hooks through the forearms**!

The Monsters are proud owners of multiple Guinness World Records titles. Burnaby hooked another one on October 25, 2011, when he hauled a truck 366 feet, 6 inches—the **farthest distance to pull a vehicle with meat hooks in the back**. The unusual feat of strength was performed with an 8,929-pound truck at the Pacific National Exhibition in Vancouver, British Columbia. Even more impressive? The vehicle was 100 pounds heavier than the minimum record requirement!

THE GREATEST STUNT DIVER

Darren Taylor knows how to make quite a splash. The diver known as Professor Splash made history on the set of *CCTV—Guinness World Records Special* in Xiamen, Fujian, China, on September 9, 2014, with the **highest shallow dive** from a height of 37 feet, 11 inches into a mere 12 inches of water. He has appeared on numerous television shows, including *America's Got Talent* and *Jimmy Kimmel Live*, and on the Discovery Channel and the History Channel. Professor Splash also holds the record for the **highest shallow dive into fire**, leaping from 26 feet, 3 inches into 10 inches of flaming water on *NBC's Show Stopping Sunday* on June 21, 2014.

SLICE AND DICE

Bet the fruit salad at your local grocery store didn't go through this! The **most melons chopped on the stomach of someone on a bed of nails** is 10. With a time limit of one minute, **Johnny Strange** used a samurai sword to slice the watermelons on the body of **Daniella D'Ville** as she lay on a bed of 400 nails at the Doncaster Tattoo Jam in South Yorkshire, UK, on October 12, 2013.

THROW DOWN

The Great Throwdini (aka Dr. David R. Adamovich of the USA) doesn't fool around when it comes to cutlery. This expert knife-thrower and holder of multiple Guinness World Records titles threw 102 14-inch knives around his daring assistant, Target Girl Tina Nagy (USA), on December 26, 2007—the **most knives thrown around a human target in one minute**. Some of the knives are on display at the Guinness World Records Museum in Niagara Falls, Ontario, Canada.

TIGHT SQUEEZE

Contortionist siblings **Skye Broberg**, **Nele Siezen**, and **Jola Siezen** apparently aren't claustrophobic. These bendy New Zealanders climbed into a box with an interior measuring just 26 by 27 by 22 inches and were able to stay inside for 6 minutes, 13.52 seconds, the **longest time spent in a box by three contortionists**. They secured the record on the TV show *NZ Smashes Guinness World Records* in Auckland, New Zealand, on September 20, 2009.

CHAPTER 2
Make 'Em Laugh: Comic Performers

Laughter makes the world go round—and can also be the path to Guinness World Records fame, as these hilarious entertainers have shown!

FUNNY BUSINESS

People love to laugh. And by the looks of **Jeff Dunham**'s "Spark of Insanity" tour, a lot of people were chuckling from September 13, 2007, to August 21, 2010. The American ventriloquist and comedian achieved the **most tickets sold for a stand-up comedy tour**, with 1,981,720 sales. The act was performed in 386 venues worldwide.

THE BEST MEDICINE

If the audience of 200 people watching **Taylor Goodwin** left with stomachaches after his performance on November 14, 2014, you couldn't blame them. That's because the Australian comedian told a whopping 550 jokes in 60 minutes: the **most jokes told in one hour**.

While **Clive Greenaway** of the UK had them rolling in the aisles at the Arts Centre in Haverhill, Suffolk, UK, on June 22, 2014, telling 26 jokes in 60 seconds: the **most jokes told in one minute**.

KIND OF A FUNNY STORY

David Scott didn't let any hecklers stand in his way on April 29 through 30, 2013. The American comedian, who goes by the name The Midnight Swinger, performed for 40 hours and 8 minutes, the **longest individual stand-up comedy show**, at the Diamond Jo Casino in Dubuque, Iowa.

NO JOKE

The yuks just kept coming at the **longest continuous stand-up comedy show by multiple comedians**. The show lasted 80 hours and was achieved by the **Laugh Factory** at their comedy club in Hollywood, California, from December 6 through 9, 2010. The show included 170 different acts by 150 comedians—it was definitely a laughing matter!

NOT SHORT ON LAUGHS

Imaan Hadchiti is the **shortest stand-up comedian**, standing 3 feet, 4.3 inches tall. Born in Australia, Imaan is of Lebanese descent and now lives in London, UK. He began his stand-up career at the age of 15 by winning the Class Clown national stand-up comedy contest in Australia. He also performed at the 2012 Edinburgh Fringe Festival and as part of the "Royal Family of Strange People" at London Wonderground in September 2012.

SEVEN-DAY STAND-UP

Australian comedian **Mark "Spud" Murphy** performed 30 shows, the **most comedy gigs in a week**, in 30 different venues around Australia, from October 14 to 20, 2007. Over the seven-day event, he helped raise more than $2,000 for the Camp Quality children's charity through ticket and T-shirt sales and donations.

CHAPTER 3
Gimme a Beat:
Music Superstars

What's that sound you hear? The sweet notes of achieving musical dreams. From a bangin' collection of drumsticks to an orchestra unlike any other, we can't stop singing these world record holders' praises!

VERSED IN RHYME

With over 124 members, the world's **largest rap group** is the hip-hop outfit **Minority Militia** of the USA. Each member of the group either rapped, sang, played an instrument, or produced on their 2001 album, *The People's Army*, released by Low Town Records.

SWEET SONG

There was music in the air on October 24, 2009. For that was the day that **Sweet Adelines International—** an organization of women barbershop-music singers based in Oklahoma—held their 63rd annual convention and earned the record for the **largest singing lesson**, with 6,651 participants. Barbershop is an American musical art form sung a cappella in four-part harmony, and the Sweet Adelines are committed to advancing barbershop harmony through education, performance, and competition. Their motto? "Harmonize the world."

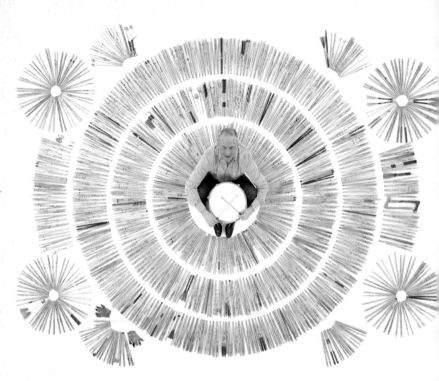

THE BEAT GOES ON

When **Peter Lavinger** caught his first drumstick from the front row of a Good Rats concert in 1980, he never imagined that 36 years later he'd be a record holder for the **largest collection of autographed drumsticks**. To date, the New Yorker has collected more than 1,300 signed drumsticks, all of which have been used by drummers representing hundreds of popular bands, including The Beatles, the Rolling Stones, Pearl Jam, and U2. The collection includes a variety of musical genres—rock, jazz, pop, and blues—and has been on display at the Hard Rock Cafe in New York City and the Rock and Roll Hall of Fame and Museum in Cleveland, Ohio.

HE LOVES THEM, YEAH, YEAH, YEAH

At the age of 10, **Rodolfo Renato Vazquez** of Argentina got The Beatles's *Rubber Soul* album—and so began a lifelong passion that goes on to this day. Rodolfo owns the **largest collection of Beatles memorabilia**—7,700 different items as of August 2011. His collection includes magazines, books, newspapers, music sheets, posters, autographs, videos, records, CDs, promotional material, stage passes, programs, concert tickets, and life-size figures of the band. The collection is so vast that it's now on display at his Beatles Museum in Buenos Aires. Rodolfo says there's no one item that he wishes he had, but there is something he'd love to do—have a cup of coffee with Paul McCartney!

CHILD'S PLAY

It's never too early to start the quest to be a world record holder. As of March 29, 2009, **Julian Pavone** was the **youngest professional drummer**. At the age of just 4 years, 10 months, 15 days, he performed his 20th concert. And since his first album, *Go Baby!*, was released by Peacock Records when he was merely 20 months old, he didn't even need to play covers. Now Julian (born May 14, 2004) plays a 22-piece custom drum set with 17 cymbals and a double kick, and attends a private school in Michigan.

HEY, MR. DJ

If you couldn't remember the name of this song written by **Mikhail Tank** of the USA, no one could blame you. It's the **longest title of a music single** and it's a mouthful at 44 words long. The title is (deep breath): "Simplify When You Get Crowded Inside, Certain Ones Prefer to Drink Your Energy, Falling Right into the Hands of Time, Release Those Who Deprive, Throw Away Ties That Bind, Just Simplify, No Need to Overextend Yourself, When They Just Rely on Your Time. No."

CATCHY, ISN'T IT?

The **longest title of a music album**, meanwhile, is American artist **Fiona Apple**'s sophomore release, *When the Pawn Hits the Conflicts He Thinks like a King What He Knows Throws the Blows When He Goes to the Fight and He'll Win the Whole Thing 'Fore He Enters the Ring There's No Body to Batter When Your Mind Is Your Might So When You Go Solo, You Hold Your Own Hand and Remember That Depth Is the Greatest of Heights and If You Know Where You Stand, Then You Know Where to Land and If You Fall It Won't Matter, Cuz You'll Know That You're Right.* Released in November 1999, it is 90 words long and is a poem that Fiona wrote after reading an unfavorable review.

MUSIC THAT'S GOOD FOR YOU

You're supposed to eat your veggies . . . but watch out that the zucchini isn't a trumpet! When it comes to fresh produce, these tomatoes and cukes have hopped off the plate and onto center stage. The **Vegetable Orchestra of Austria** uses a wide range of vegetables, like carrots (flutes!) and pumpkins (drums!) to produce its unique sounds, and performed 77 concerts in venues worldwide from 1998 to 2012, the **most concerts by a group playing vegetable instruments**. The orchestra has toured the world with their produce, performing in countries such as China, the USA, Russia, Denmark, and the Netherlands. The musicians give some of their instruments away to the audience after a performance, and also dish out soup made from the vegetables left over after preparing their instruments.

A "REEDY" LONG TIME

No one is more at home in an orchestra than **Stanley Drucker** of the USA. Born in Brooklyn, New York, Stanley holds the world record for the **longest career as a clarinetist**. He performed professionally for 62 years, 7 months, 1 day as of June 4, 2009. He began studying the clarinet at age 10, and after attending the High School of Music and Art in New York (now known as Fiorello H. LaGuardia High School of Music & Art and Performing Arts), his talent was undeniable. After performing with the Indianapolis Symphony Orchestra, the Adolf Busch Chamber Players, and the Buffalo Philharmonic, Stanley joined the New York Philharmonic in 1948. His first performance there was the New York Philharmonic's 4,616th concert. When he retired in 2009, his last show was the Philharmonic's 14,846th concert.

HE'S GOT GROOVE

If **Jeff Aug** had to pause for a moment to remember what country he was in, you couldn't blame him. As part of his Raw Fingers and Steel Strings Tour, the American guitarist toured through Luxembourg, Belgium, the Netherlands, Germany, France, Italy, Switzerland, Liechtenstein, and Austria on March 3, 2012, the **most concerts performed in different countries in 24 hours**.

MISSION COMPLETED

Jeff Aug did it again!

9 shows in 9 countries in 24 hours

Sourobhee Debbarma became the first female *Indian Idol* winner on the show's fourth season in India. But she might be best remembered as the singer with the **longest time to sing suspended upside down**. She broke the existing record by singing for 4 minutes, 35.39 seconds on February 11, 2011.

TOURS DE FORCE

German rock group **Weltrekorder** holds the world record for the **most concerts performed in 12 hours**. The band performed 35 concerts and played at venues across Cologne, Germany, on August 21 and 22, 2010. The first concert started on August 21 at 4:00 pm, and the last ended at 3:58 a.m.

The **most concerts performed in 24 hours**, meanwhile, is 65 and was achieved by Norwegian musicians **Helge Toft** (pictured) with **Jens Rimau**, **Paul Inge Vikingstad**, and **Anders Bjelland**, at venues in and around the city of Haugesund, Norway, from June 21 to 22, 2012.

ROCK AROUND THE CLOCK

To celebrate the release of his new album *Storyline*, US country singer **Hunter Hayes** undertook the **most live concerts performed in 24 hours in multiple cities**. Over May 9 through 10, 2014, he visited 10 cities: Boston, Massachusetts; Worcester, Massachusetts; Providence, Rhode Island; New London, Connecticut; New Haven, Connecticut; Stamford, Connecticut; South Orange, New Jersey; Asbury Park, New Jersey; and Philadelphia, Pennsylvania. The tour also raised funds for Feeding America.

The longest performance on a hand drum was 501 hours and was achieved by Kuzhalmannam Ramakrishnan (India) at the Rhythm Therapy Hall, Nandavanam Hospital, Ottapalam, Kerala, India, on 5-26 July 2009

STAYING POWER

If you had a ticket to see **Kuzhalmannam Ramakrishnan** at the Rhythm Therapy Hall in India in July 2009, you definitely got your money's worth. That's because the performer gave the **longest concert by a solo artist**. He started the performance on July 5 and ended on July 26! Let's hope he took some breaks for food, water, and the bathroom!

And guess what? The same event also earned Kuzhalmannam the record for **longest marathon hand drumming**—clocking a staggering time of 501 hours.

Stunts and tricks seem to come naturally to the folks you'll meet on these pages. They've proven that when it comes to attempting to break a world record, they have the skills to lasso the moon!

TIMBER HO-HO-HO!

When it comes to Christmas trees, **Erin Lavoie** really has the holiday spirit! This world-class athlete from Spokane, Washington, holds the record for **most Christmas trees chopped in two minutes**, felling 27 trees on December 19, 2008, in Germany. Erin is a CrossFit athlete and competes in Lumberjack Sports, which includes various events such as wood chopping, log rolling, and axe throwing!

In 2006, at just seven years old, **Maxwell William Mobley** (pictured) became the **youngest person to compete in the Wild West Arts contest** when he took part in the youth wedding ring race. It involves running a race while maintaining a rope loop around the body. Maxwell competed at the Will Rogers Wild West International Expo in Claremore, Oklahoma.

TEXAS-SIZE TALENT

At 11 years old, **Cody Lamb** is the **youngest person to win the Wild West Arts Texas skip race** at the Will Rogers Wild West International Expo in Oklahoma in 2006. And skills run in the family at Cody's house: Cody; his mother, Kim; and his father, Dan, were all inducted into the National Knife Throwers Hall of Fame in Austin, Texas, in 2007 as the Western Performing Family of the Year.

SHORTEST STUNTMAN

At 4 feet, 1.7 inches, **Kiran Shah** has reached towering heights when it comes to the world of stunts. The British actor is the **shortest professional stuntman** currently working in films, appearing in 52 movies since 1976 and performing stunts in 31 of them. He was the perspective stunt double for Christopher Reeve in *Superman* and *Superman 2,* and more recently Elijah Wood in the *Lord of the Rings* trilogy.

NERVES OF STEEL

Roy Alon knows his way around a movie set. Since beginning his stunt career in 1968, the Brit has worked on a whopping 937 television, film, and theater productions as a stunt coordinator, performer, or second unit director as of May 10, 2005, making him the **most-prolific TV, film, and theater stuntman**.

ULTIMATE FACT:

A Texas skip is a vertical loop that is repeatedly pulled from one side of the body to the other. With each pass, the roper jumps through the center of the loop.

TEXAS SKIP

American **Andrew Rotz** broke the previous record of **most consecutive Texas-style skips** at the National Convention of the Wild West Arts Club in Las Vegas, Nevada, on March 11, 2003. In 3 hours, 10 minutes, he achieved 11,123 Texas skips in a row, smashing the previous record set at 4,011.

ALL TIED UP

Charlie Keyes of the USA (pictured) earns his place as a Guinness World Records holder with the **largest trick-roping loop**. He spun a loop around him fed to a length of 107 feet, 2 inches at the Will Rogers International Wild West Expo in Claremore, Oklahoma, on April 22, 2006. The **female** holder of this record is **Kimberley Mink** also from the USA, who spun a loop around her fed to a length of 76 feet, 2 inches, at Jerome High School in Idaho, on January 25, 2003.

CHAPTER 5
It's Magic!

Some Guinness World Records feats are so unbelievable that you might think magic was involved. In this chapter, you'd be right! Get ready to be enchanted by the achievements in this supernaturally

BUNNY BONANZA

When Italian magicians **Walter Rolfo** and **Piero Ustignani**—otherwise known as Jabba—began pulling rabbits out of a top hat during the Magic Congress in Saint-Vincent, Italy, on May 17, 2008, they didn't stop at one. Or 10. Or even 50! Nope, the duo didn't stop producing fluffy tails and floppy ears until they had pulled out 300 bunnies, the **most rabbits pulled out of a hat**.

SHATTERED GLASS

Walter Rolfo and **Piero Ustignani** haven't shattered just one world record. They needed brooms and dustbins to clean up all the broken glass at the Masters of Magic convention at the Casino de la Vallee in Saint-Vincent, Italy, on April 15, 2011. That was the day they achieved the **most glasses broken during a mind-control stage illusion**. A table with 140 standard wine glasses was used for the trick, and a total of 66 glasses were broken.

MAGIC UNITES

Israeli magician **Israel Cagliostro Oxman** taught 1,476 students a card trick on June 1, 2015, as part of the world's **largest magic lesson**. The event—called "Haifa Magic for Peace"—was held in Haifa, Israel, and not only set out to break a record but also to encourage cross-cultural interaction by bringing together Muslim, Jewish, and Christian students.

A BIG CLASS

La Fundación Abracadabra de Magos Solidarios of Spain was able to take credit for the **largest magic lesson in multiple locations** on December 10, 2010. In total, 2,573 people took part in a magic class held simultaneously at different venues. The lesson included two tricks: the sudden wand and the cut and restored bandage.

A MAGICAL MINUTE

Performing one magic trick in a minute takes skill. But 17 tricks? While not being able to see anything? In 2011, that was enough to earn **Fernando Diaz** (pictured) from Venezuela the record for **most magic tricks performed blindfolded in one minute**. More amazing still, Fernando has since been surpassed by British magician **Clive Greenaway**, who achieved 18 tricks in the same time in 2015.

The **largest card illusion reveal** measured 1,380 square feet. It was performed by Italian PhD student **Danilo Audiello**, aka Alexis Arts, using a projection artwork created with Ross Ashton of the UK on an exterior wall at the University of Cambridge, UK, on February 22, 2014. Alexis is constantly setting new goals, and has said, "If you are able to amaze someone, your work has meaning."

CHAPTER 6
Can't Stop Dancing!

Did you know you can dance your way into Guinness World Records glory? Time to lace up your pointe shoes and meet the dancers who kicked, twirled, and waltzed to the top of the heap.

QUITE AN ENSEMBLE

At an **America Sings!** Festival in Long Beach, California, 1,628 participants danced a routine choreographed by John Jacobson to the song "Because We Sing" on April 3, 2004. This vocal extravaganza earned them the record for the **most people in a chorus line**.

BARRE NONE

On May 22, 2011, at the Orange County Convention Center in Orlando, Florida, 245 dancers from the **Dr. Phillips High School Dance Magnet**, the **Orlando Ballet**, and other local dance schools supported their body weight on the tips of their toes—en pointe—for a full minute, the **most ballet dancers en pointe**. As the 60 seconds ticked by, some of the dancers were getting fatigued, but Emily Cordell, a teacher at Dr. Phillips who was leading the group, shouted encouragement. And when the minute was over, the dancers' heels came down and a shout went out to confirm they had set the world record!

TWIRL, BALLERINA, TWIRL

This Chinese husband and wife team stands head and shoulders above the rest! **Wu Zhengdan** balances in arabesque on her husband **Wei Baohua**'s head before performing classical ballet pirouettes en pointe. On the set of *Lo Show dei Record* in Rome, Italy, on March 28, 2012, she achieved four twirls, the **most pirouettes en pointe on the head**. One secret to their success? Wei Baohua wears a cap with a small groove in it for his wife to position her pointe shoe.

A LIFELONG PASSION

Grete Brunvoll of Norway hasn't let age stop her from dancing. The **oldest performing ballerina** was born July 27, 1930, and began dancing at the age of six. Her first professional performance was when she was 15 years old, and as she entered her 80s, she still trained every day and made regular public performances.

DANCE MAN

The **oldest competitive ballroom dancer** is **Frederick Salter** of the UK. Born on February 13, 1911, Salter passed his IDTA Gold Bar Level 3 examinations in Latin and ballroom with honors at the age of 100 years, 245 days, in London, UK, on October 15, 2011. He performed the rumba, cha-cha, samba, and *paso* dances for his Latin examination, and the waltz, quickstep, tango, and foxtrot for ballroom, achieving a score of 99.75 out of 100 in both categories.

TRACK RECORD

David Turner and **Katie Walton** of the UK danced into the record books on April 7, 2013. They covered 5.03 miles, the **farthest distance danced by a couple**, at Hadley Stadium Athletics Track in Birmingham, UK. Competitive ballroom and Latin dancers, David and Katie teamed up for the record attempt, during which they performed different styles of ballroom dancing, including the quickstep, foxtrot, American smooth, and waltz.

MASTERS OF LATIN

British dancing duo **Donnie Burns** and **Gaynor Fairweather**, both MBEs (Members of the Order of the British Empire), have performed tangos, cha-chas, rumbas, and beyond to earn the record for **most successful Latin American dancing partnership**. During their dancing career, they have won 14 World Latin titles, including the World Professional Latin Championship 13 times in a row, and remain undefeated anywhere in the world since 1983.

DANCE TILL YOU DROP

There was no time to stop and rest on November 15 to 16, 2008, for Mexican dance partners **Francisco Petatán-Garcia** and **Joana Salinas-Aviles**. That's because the professional dancers were in the middle of the **longest dance marathon by a couple**, for which they boogied nonstop for 35 hours!

WHAT'S YOUR NAME AGAIN?

No one could blame **Michael Hull** of Germany if he forgot his dance partners' names on November 23 and 24, 2007. That's because he achieved the record for **most dance partners in 24 hours**, twirling, spinning, and gliding with 1,068 people!

GLIDING BY

Blink and you might miss the **fastest 20-meter** (65-foot) **moonwalk**: it took **Ashiq Baluch** of the UK (pictured) only 6.53 seconds on October 17, 2013, to complete the famous dance move pioneered by Michael Jackson, which gives the illusion of being pulled backward while attempting to walk forward.

The **fastest 100-meter** (328-foot) **moonwalk**, meanwhile, took a mere 32.06 seconds and was achieved by China's **Luo Lantu** on the set of *Guinness World Records Special* in Beijing, China, on December 8, 2010.

DISCO FEVER

The **largest disco ball** in the world measures 33 feet, 10 inches in diameter—taller than most houses! It was used at **Bestival**'s Desert Island Disco festival held on the Isle of Wight, UK, on September 7, 2014.

DAZZLING DANCERS

If you're a fan of Irish music and dance, Dublin, the capital city of Ireland, was the place to be on July 21, 2013. At an event organized by **Abhann Productions**, 1,693 participants formed the **longest "Riverdance" line**. Irish step dancers are famed for their fast-moving feet and legs, while the arms and upper torso remain still.

BOOT-SCOOTIN' GIRL

Siobhan Dunn of the UK won the Junior World Line Dance Championship in Nashville, Tennessee, on January 10, 1998, at the age of 6 years, 194 days, making her the **youngest world line-dance champion**.

But country wasn't the only type of dance Siobhan had a talent for. She made the leap to swing dancing and came in fourth place in the junior youth division at the 2000 US Open.

TAP WHIZ

Quick-footed **Rosario Varela** of Spain attained 1,274 taps in a minute on the set of *Guinness World Records* in Madrid, Spain, on January 23, 2009, making her the **fastest female flamenco dancer**.

FAST AND CLEAN

The **most break-dance windmills performed in 30 seconds** is . . . 50! In this move, the break-dancer rolls the torso nonstop in a circular path on the floor and twirls their legs in a V shape. This record was set by **Mauro Peruzzi** of Italy, aka Cico, at the Sony Ericsson UK B-Boy Championships World Finals in London, UK, on October 10, 2010.

HOP TO IT

Break-dancer **Benedikt Mordstein** of Germany achieved the **most consecutive elbow hops**—66!—in celebration of Guinness World Records Day in 2011.

SHE SPINS HEAD SPINS

The female record for **most head spins in one minute** is 101 and was achieved by **Roxanne Milliner** of the UK (pictured), aka B-girl Roxie, on the set of *Officially Amazing* in Edinburgh, Scotland, UK, on July 18, 2013.

The **most consecutive head spins by a female**, meanwhile, is 47, set by dancer **Luisa Asbeck** from Germany on November 13, 2014. Roxanne and Luisa must have felt dizzy with success after their spinathons!

FLARED UP

The **most break-dance virgin air flares in one minute** is 39 and was achieved by **Junior Bosila Banya**, aka B-Boy Junior, of France at the Sony Ericsson UK B-Boy Championships World Finals in London, UK, on October 10, 2010. A virgin air flare is like a standard air flare except the legs are closed instead of in a V shape. It is sometimes referred to as a Thomas flare—the name used for a similar move in gymnastics.

HIPS DON'T LIE

The first time **Melanie White** of Australia attempted the record for **longest belly-dance shimmy**, it did not go well: owing to a technical failure with the camera equipment, her attempt could not be verified. But that didn't stop Melanie! She went on to achieve the record at the Moruya Live Life Expo in Riverside Park, Moruya, Australia, on February 25, 2012. She shimmied for 3 hours, 7 seconds, promoting belly-dancing as a performance art of great physical skill and cultural depth.

FLAMENCO FEAT

November 2, 2012, was the day a dream came true for Spanish dancer **Israel Vivancos**, of the flamenco dance company Los Vivancos. For on that day in Madrid, he achieved the **most flamenco taps in one minute**—1,317. The fast footwork Israel performed during the attempt was the toe-heel technique.

Los Vivancos is an extreme flamenco fusion group composed of seven brothers, Elías, Josué, Josua, Cristo, Aarón, Judah, and of course Israel, who perform worldwide. The brothers have said that they've followed Guinness World Records with "wonder and astonishment" since they were children, and have always dreamed of becoming record holders themselves.

SWING YOUR PARTNER

Student organization the **Cowboy Country Swing Club**, from the University of Wyoming, gathered 1,184 swingers on April 30, 2015, to claim the record for **largest swing dance**.

ULTIMATE FACT:
The most famous swing dance is the Lindy Hop—which started in the 1920s—and it's still danced today!

TOP TAPPERS

Running 32 miles isn't easy—but **Danny Meenan** of the USA didn't just run it, he *tapped* it—the **longest distance tap-danced**. The tapping marathon took him 7 hours, 35 minutes at the Count Basie Track and Field in Red Bank, New Jersey, on October 8, 2001.

Angell Husted of Palmyra, Virginia, set the **female** record by dancing 20 miles, 189 feet in eight hours at the Fluvanna County High School Gym on May 8, 1999.

DEVINE INSPIRATION

Blink and you'll miss **James Devine**'s fantastic footwork. The Irishman holds the Guinness World Records title for the **fastest tap dance**—achieving 38 taps in just a second at the MCM recording studios in Sydney, Australia, on May 25, 1998. In fact, his tapping feet were so fast that they had to be recorded by a computer to provide the final count.

GET YOUR TAP SHOES ON

On May 24, 1998, a record 6,951 tap dancers gathered to perform the **largest tap dance**, at the City Square in Stuttgart, Germany. The routine, choreographed by **Ray Lynch** of the USA, lasted 2 minutes, 25 seconds, and was to a tune called "Klicke-di-Klack" that Ray composed himself.

KEEP ON TAPPING

On March 22, 2002, a total of 7,596 children from 40 London schools in the UK simultaneously tap-danced for five minutes to the song "To the Show," achieving the **largest tap dance in multiple venues**. The event was organized by the **North London Performing Arts Center**.

GIVE ME AN R-E-C-O-R-D!

Get ready to root for a new group of record holders.
The **largest cheerleading dance** was achieved by
1,371 people at an event to celebrate the 20th anniversary
of **Wing Dance Promotion Co., Ltd.** in Japan on
August 30, 2015. This smashed the previous record by
1,074 cheerleaders—now that's something to cheer about!

CAN, CAN, CANCAN

The **most demi-grand *rond de jambe* cancan kicks by a chorus line** is 29 kicks in 30 seconds and was achieved by the dancers of the **Moulin Rouge** in Paris, France, for Guinness World Records Day on November 7, 2014.

The Moulin Rouge is a world-famous cabaret in Paris, and its red windmill on the roof is an iconic image in the city. Known as the birthplace of the cancan, the Moulin Rouge continues to entertain thousands of visitors from around the globe every year.

DANCE OF THE PEOPLE

The **largest bamboo dance** (also known as *cheraw*) was achieved by 10,736 dancers during an event organized by the **local government of Aizawl**, Mizoram, India, on March 12, 2010.

The *cheraw* is a very colorful and distinctive dance performed with great precision and elegance. Dancers move by stepping alternately in and out from between and across a pair of horizontal bamboo canes, held against the ground by people sitting face-to-face on either side. They tap the bamboo in rhythm, and when clapped, the canes produce a sound that forms the beat of the dance. The patterns and steps of the dance generate many vibrations. Sometimes the moves are made to imitate birds and the swaying of trees.

SENIOR SALSA

Sarah Paddy Jones is the **oldest acrobatic salsa dancer**. The Brit was born July 1, 1934, and won first prize on the Spanish TV talent show *Tú Sí Que Vales* in December 2009. She was awarded her Guinness World Records title on the set of Italian TV show *Lo Show dei Record* on March 4, 2010, at the age of 75.

SAMBA ON

The **largest samba dance** took place on June 15, 2014, in Bangkok, Thailand, in order to promote the **Tesco Lotus** hypermarket. For three minutes, 525 dancers danced Zambaro-bic, a fusion of Brazilian samba and Zumba aerobics.

SPLASH TO THE LEFT

Not just one but three Guinness World Records were achieved by participants at **LeapFrog**'s National Fit Made Fun Day held in Santa Monica, California, on September 6, 2014. Led by former USA women's national soccer team captain Mia Hamm, one of the records was for the **largest swim dance** (pictured), for which 318 people took the plunge!

ULTIMATE FACT:
The **longest aerobics marathon** was 39 hours, 20 minutes, and was performed by Esther Featherstone of the UK in September 2012!

HANDS IN THE AIR

In 2013, **Bryan Nguyen** (pictured) achieved the **most jackhammer hops in one minute**, with a total of 49. The bar has since been raised even higher by German break-dancer **Benedikt Mordstein**, who completed 63 on April 12, 2015—that's more than one per second!

CHAPTER 7
Teamwork

Nothing feels better than working with a group of people toward a common goal. And for the acclaimed assemblages in this chapter, their combined efforts paid off handsomely. Whether swimming together, crowding into a tiny car, or even dressing up, these collaborations prove that sometimes all you need to achieve greatness is a little help from your friends.

264 DALMATIANS

On July 14, 2014, 264 people "woofed" it up. **Thistley Hough Academy** in Stoke on Trent, UK, set the world record for **largest gathering of people dressed as dogs**. Children at the school dressed up as Dalmatians by wearing black-and-white costumes and having their faces painted. Such a crowd must have been quite easy to *spot*!

BUTTERFLY STROKES

The **most participants in a swimathon** were the 4,546 people who took part in a one-hour-long charity event organized by the **Rotary Club of Grantham** in Lincolnshire, UK, on February 25, 2012. The swimathon took place at more than 64 locations across the world between 12:00 and 1:00 p.m. GMT. The swimmers' mission? To help eradicate polio worldwide.

THE GUY IN THE RED-AND-WHITE-STRIPED SHIRT

Where's Waldo? That was the question nobody had to ask on June 19, 2011, in Dublin, Ireland. Why? Because he was everywhere! The **largest gathering of people dressed as Waldo** was achieved at the Street Performance World Championship, with 3,872 Waldos earning their stripes!

PUPPET GIANTS

On July 6, 2003, 215 papier-mâché giants made by 88 organizations gathered for the third annual meeting of the **Colla Gegantera del Carnaval de Solsona** in Catalonia, Spain—the **most people dressed in giant papier-mâché puppets**.

The giants tend to take the forms of royal figures. Their origins are unknown, although many European countries have adopted the tradition of having them dance down the streets as part of festival celebrations. In Catalonia, the earliest known records are from the 14th century, when biblical characters David and Goliath were created as part of the procession of the feast of Corpus Christi in Barcelona, Spain.

GIMME 20

Marines are known for their toughness—and apparently their upper arm strength! On September 18, 2013, the **Single Marine Program Camp Lejeune** in Jacksonville, North Carolina, took the world record for **most people performing a chain push-up** as 138 Marines and sailors linked themselves together, their legs resting on the shoulders of the person behind them, and completed three push-ups. This wasn't a spur-of-the-moment drill—it was five months in the making!

WATCH YOUR ELBOW

Smart cars aren't known for their roominess, but on the set of *Guinness World Records Gone Wild,* 20 members of the **Glendale Cheerleading Team** of the USA (pictured) climbed into one, the **most people in a smart car**. This record was equaled by the **Comets Cheerleaders** on the set of *Lo Show dei Record* in Italy, on July 3, 2014.

PLATE UP!

The **most people spinning plates simultaneously** was 1,026 at the official opening of the **Sportcampus** in Utrecht, Netherlands, on September 25, 2007.

LET'S (CLAP) BREAK A RECORD!

If you were near the Sun National Bank Arena in Trenton, New Jersey, on November 12, 2011, you might have heard the **largest cheerleading cheer**. In the arena, 1,278 cheerleaders from **Science Cheerleaders** and **Pop Warner** lent their voice to the record attempt as part of a regional competition.

WAVE A FLAG

Using flags and pennants to send signals was all part of the day's events at the Hong Kong Stadium in China on November 21, 2010. With 23,321 members of the **Scout Association** taking part, spelling out "HKS100," a new record was set for **most people performing flag signals**.

CHAPTER 8
You Say Juggle,
I Say Joggle

A round of applause for this group of Guinness World Records stars, who have tossed balls, apples, and even tires in order to claim their spots in the record books!

IN THE AIR

For two years, **Alex Barron** of the UK practiced juggling in order to attempt the **most balls juggled**, a record that had not been broken for 16 years! On April 3, 2012, at age 18, he spent four and a half hours at Roehampton Squash Club in London, UK, trying to reach his target. He was beginning to get tired when, finally, he juggled 11 balls and managed 23 consecutive catches in what is known as a qualifying juggling run! Alex also jointly holds the record for **most balls flashed by a juggler**, although for his attempt he used beanbags, achieving one throw better than a 12-ball flash, with a total of 13 throws.

MUSCLE UP

Circus strongman **Denys Ilchenko** from Ukraine showed why his nickname is Hercules on July 17, 2013. He earned the record for **greatest weight juggled** by juggling three car tires weighing a combined 59 pounds, 7.6 ounces on the set of *Officially Amazing* in the UK.

JOGGLING MASTERS

As if juggling isn't tricky enough, some people like to juggle while jogging—or "joggle." **Eric Walter** of the USA knows how to keep things moving—he holds the Guinness World Records title for the **fastest 400 meters** (1,312 feet) **joggling with three objects**, clocking 55.81 seconds at the Bowling Green State University track in Ohio, on July 20, 2013.

The female record for **fastest five kilometers** (3.1 miles) **joggling with three objects** is 20 minutes, 40 seconds, by **Dana Guglielmo** (USA) at Cooper River Park in Pennsauken, New Jersey, on April 6, 2014.

SERIOUS SKILLS

Emil Faltynek of the Czech Republic used a ladder to reach his world record! He achieved the **longest duration juggling five objects balanced on a ladder footplate**, lasting 56.92 seconds in Kairouan, Tunisia, on March 23, 2013.

WATCH YOUR STEP

The **greatest distance traveled on a slackline while juggling three objects**, meanwhile, is 109 feet, 4.99 inches, and was achieved by South African juggler **Lyle Bennett** at the Wild Clover Farm in Stellensbosch, South Africa, on October 4, 2014.

BALLS IN THE AIR

In juggling, a backcross involves throwing an object from one hand so it passes behind the juggler's back to be caught in front of the body by the opposite hand, then throwing it again around the back to the first hand. The **most consecutive backcross juggling catches with seven balls** is 69 (75 throws), achieved by 14-year-old **Ty Tojo** of the USA on February 25, 2013, while practicing in Las Vegas, Nevada.

WHAT A CATCH!

The **most juggling catches of three balls in one minute** is 422, achieved by **Zdeněk Bradáč** of the Czech Republic, in the Czech capital, Prague, on February 8, 2012.

BUZZ-WORTHY

The **most chain saw–juggling catches** is 94 and was achieved by Canadian **Ian Stewart** in Windsor, Nova Scotia, Canada, on September 25, 2011. During his attempt, Ian used three Zenoah G2000T chain saws weighing 4.85 pounds each. The chain saws were fully engaged during the attempt, which lasted for 37 seconds. More recently, on August 21, 2014, Ian also earned the record for **most consecutive axe-juggling catches** with 580 catches!

BIG BITE

The **most bites taken from three apples while juggling** is 151 in a minute and was achieved by **Michael Goudeau** of the USA on *Guinness World Records Unleashed* in Los Angeles, California, on June 20, 2013.

FEET FIRST

Balls aren't the only items that can be juggled—and you don't always have to use your hands either. US circus performer **Chester Cable** juggled an aluminum table weighing 130 pounds with his feet 17 times in succession on October 16, 1998—the **most consecutive foot-juggling flips of a table**.

HANGING OUT

Being upside down didn't stop **Quinn Spicker** of Canada from achieving his dream of setting a Guinness World Records title. He spent the **longest duration juggling three objects while suspended upside down**, lasting 12 minutes, 50 seconds at the PNE Garden Auditorium in Vancouver, British Columbia, Canada, on July 22, 2010.

MARATHON JOGGLER

Spectators at the Scotiabank Toronto Waterfront Marathon on September 30, 2007, witnessed history as Canadian runner **Michal Kapral** completed the 26.22 miles while juggling three balls in 2 hours, 50 minutes, 12 seconds—the **fastest marathon while joggling three objects**. Michal also holds the title for **fastest half-marathon joggling with three objects (male)**, completing it in 1 hour, 20 minutes, 40 seconds at the same marathon on October 19, 2014.

PEDAL POWER

Jonathan Oberlerchner of Austria first rode a unicycle when he was eight years old. Eight years later, on July 25, 2013, he traveled the **farthest distance on a unicycle while juggling three objects**—15,764 feet— at Leopold Wagner Arena in Klagenfurt, Austria.

CHAPTER 9
Random Acts of Greatness

Some Guinness World Records are so bizarre that they defy categorization. As the final curtain of this book of performing greats draws to a close, be prepared to have your mind blown by a matchless group of record-breakers.

NO STOPPING THEM

Escaping from a straitjacket seems impossible on its own—but what if you were suspended in the air? Ask **Scott Hammell** of Canada how it feels! On August 13, 2003, Scott escaped from a straitjacket while suspended from a 50-foot rope hanging below the basket of a hot-air balloon 7,200 feet over Knoxville, Tennessee. It's the **highest suspension straitjacket escape** to date.

Straitjackets don't faze **James Peters** from the UK either. He holds the record for **most straitjacket escapes in eight hours**, getting out 193 times in Chelmsford, Essex, UK, on September 27, 2003. His fastest escape was achieved in just 56 seconds!

What's the **fastest escape from a straitjacket in suspension without chains**? An unbelievable 8.40 seconds. It was achieved by Canadian **Lucas Wilson** at a high school in Ontario, Canada, on June 8, 2012. Lucas used a Green Posey straitjacket and was suspended in the air by his ankles.

ARRESTING DEVELOPMENT

The **most handcuff escapes in 24 hours** is 10,625 and was achieved on February 12 to 13, 2010, by multi-record holder **Zdeněk Bradáč** in Liberec, Czech Republic. Considering he averaged 442 escapes every hour, it's safe to say Zdeněk didn't show much "restraint" when he took on this challenge.

GRAB IT!

Australian record-breaker **Anthony Kelly** had to keep his eyes peeled on November 13, 2014, to catch the **most spears from a spear gun underwater**. He caught 10 spears in one minute while in a swimming pool at Sports UNE in New South Wales, Australia. This beat the previous record by three spears.

FIRE OUT!

The **most candles extinguished with a braided ponytail** is 26, achieved by **Anuradha I. Mandal**, aka Rimpi, of India, on the set of *Guinness World Records— Ab India Todega* on February 11, 2011. That girl's on fire!

American balloon artist **John Cassidy** (pictured) must be in demand at birthday parties. The magician and balloon master was able to make 747 balloon shapes in Newtown, Pennsylvania, on November 14, 2007— the **most balloon sculptures made in one hour**. Growing up, John wondered what it would be like to be a record-breaker—and then he made it happen!

Meanwhile, fellow balloon modeler **Tim Thurmond** of the US can churn out thousands of balloon sculptures. On April 16 and 17, 2004, Tim made 6,176 sculptures—the **most balloon sculptures in 24 hours**!

DON'T LOOK NOW

On November 20, 2007, **Daniele Bottalico** of Italy, aka Mago Ciccio, made a balloon poodle using a single modeling balloon in 4.54 seconds. What's more, he did it without being able to see it. That's the **fastest time to make a modeling-balloon dog behind the back**.

JAILHOUSE ROCKED

No one can ever compare to the King. But **Victor Beasley** of Belgium came close with the **longest career as an Elvis impersonator**. He performed as Elvis Presley from 1955 right through to his death in 2003. During the course of his career, Victor was made an honorary citizen of Tupelo, Mississippi, the birthplace of Elvis Presley.

GAMER'S PARADISE

At the 2010 Isle of Wight Festival, 16,000 people gathered to watch not a band but . . . a video game. It was the **largest audience for a video game performance** and was achieved by *ZOO Magazine*'s **Matt Beadle** and Activision's **Jon Edney**, who played the music game *DJ Hero*.

SAY (GURGLE) AHHHHH

Opening your mouth underwater is difficult enough, but can you imagine swallowing swords at the same time? Australian **Chayne Hultgren**, aka Space Cowboy, swallowed four, the **most swords swallowed underwater**, on the set of *Lo Show dei Record* on July 11, 2014. Chayne had the blades bound together before swallowing them, as it's only possible to attempt the record with one breath.

EN GARDE!

The late **Christopher Lee** holds the title for **most screen swordfights by an actor**, having duelled in 17 films with foils, swords, lightsabers, and even billiard cues!

MAESTRO OF MAKEUP

American makeup artist **Rick Baker** is responsible for some of the most iconic characters ever to grace the cinematic screen. He can boast the **most Oscar wins for makeup** in the history of the Academy Awards. His first Oscar was for *An American Werewolf in London* (1981), and his most recent was for *The Wolfman* (2011). Some of his other Oscar-winning films are *The Nutty Professor*, *Men in Black*, and *Dr. Seuss's How the Grinch Stole Christmas*.

CAN YOU PAINT A . . . ?

It was a blur of paintbrushes and face paint at **The Big Moo** music festival in Milton Keynes, UK, on June 23, 2007, as 607 faces were painted in one hour: the **most faces painted in one hour by a team of five**. This bettered the record by 24 faces.

HE STAYED FOR THE CREDITS

Spending an entire day watching movies sounds fun, doesn't it? Well, **Ashish Sharma** of India spent over five days (120 hours, 23 minutes) at the KDDC Movie Theater in Mathura, India, watching 48 films, the **longest marathon watching movies**. He did take rest breaks in between each showing, but none of these exceeded 10 minutes.

SMILE FOR THE CAMERA

While most toddlers are busy learning their ABCs, **Rirenda Shrestha** from Nepal was figuring out his next shot. The world's **youngest professional photographer** was only 2 years, 2 days old when he exhibited and sold his work at the Nepal Art Council from December 31, 2006, to January 3, 2007. The exhibit was titled *Nepal through the Eyes of a Young Photographer*.

GROUNDHOG PLAY

If you had a ticket to the **27 O'Clock Players'** performance of *The Bald Soprano* by Eugene Ionesco on July 17, 2010, you needed to pack *a lot* of snacks. That's because it was the **longest continuous dramatic performance** on record, lasting 23 hours, 33 minutes, 54 seconds. Eugene's play has a looped ending, and the plot requires the continuous repetition of the play with the actors swapping roles. During this record-breaking performance, the script was repeated 25 times!

AN EPIC PROJECT

The **largest entertainment voice-over project** was undertaken for the creation of the LucasArts video game *Star Wars: The Old Republic* (released in 2011). More than 200,000 lines of recorded voice-over dialogue were performed by several hundred voice actors for the MMORPG (massively multiplayer online role-playing game).

The audio team spent several thousand hours recording dialogue—the longest recording time for any video game, film, or TV program. By comparison, most feature-film screenplays contain fewer than 1,000 lines of dialogue

GUITAR GODS

Zac "The Magnet" Monro (pictured) of the UK and **Ochi "Dainoj" Yosuke** of Japan share the **most Air Guitar World Championship wins**: they've each claimed the title twice at the Music Video Festival's Air Guitar World Championships, held annually in Finland.

JETÉ IN THE JETS

Kathryn Pounder and **Rebecca MacEnri**, both from the UK, set the world record for the **most ballet leg switches while synchronized swimming**: 71 in a minute. They achieved this on November 9, 2006, in the Trafalgar Square fountains in central London as part of the Guinness World Records Day celebrations.